A SIMPLE EXPLANATION OF PRAYER

CONCORDIA PUBLISHING HOUSE · SAINT LOUIS

3558 S. Jefferson Ave.
St. Louis, MO 63118-3968

1-800-325-3040 • cph.org

Written by Daniel Paavola

Manufactured in the United States of America

1 2 3 4 5 6 7 8 9 10 31 30 29 28 27 26 25 24 23 22

CONVERSATION WITH GOD

Prayer is our conversation with God, a conversation built on His mercy and commands. It is a remarkable bridge that spans heaven and earth, connecting our tiny lives with our Lord in heaven. Yet who are we, sinful and insignificant as we are, to talk with the mighty and eternal God? We're children of the heavenly Father, commanded to speak and thrilled at the privilege.

The bridge of prayer is built on God's words and gracious promises. Prayer brings us into the continuous heavenly conversation that is already going on.

In the conversation of prayer, we tell God our hopes and fears, our flaws and desires, confident that He cares deeply about them all. We acknowledge the many promises He has made to us. He listens intently to our words, though He knows them all before we speak and has already prepared His answer. Our prayers echo the words Jesus has already spoken for us. Romans 8:34 tells us He "indeed is interceding for us" with the Father. Our Mediator prayed, "I do not ask for these only, but also for those who will believe in Me" (John 17:20). Even when we are unable to find words, we pray because the Holy Spirit "intercedes for us with groanings too deep for words" (Romans 8:26).

It's only by His mercy that we dare approach Him. Because of Christ's death and resurrection, we know God has already forgiven us so we can come into His presence with confidence.

God Commands Us to Pray

Parents are thrilled to hear their child's first word. Those same parents, years later, ask that same child, "How was school?" and love the engaging conversation that follows. Young people on their first date are thrilled to talk with each other effortlessly for hours. That same couple, married for sixty years, still hasn't stopped talking.

People need to talk. Sometimes conversation begins by design, but more often it occurs as the result of the simple, natural act of being together. This can be a model of prayer. In our relationship with God, the conversation of prayer happens by His command and by His invitation. It's also our time to remember His Word and to repeat those words and promises back to Him. Our joyful discovery is that He listens to us and welcomes our words.

With the firmness of a Father and Creator, God commands us to pray. He commands us to use His name rightly, and we do so when we pray to Him. He provides us the very words to say in the Lord's Prayer: He tells us, "When you pray, say . . ." (Luke 11:2). His command to pray includes His promise to answer: "Ask, and it will be given to you; seek, and you will find; knock, and it will be opened to you" (Luke 11:9). God knows that we most often pray when we're in need, so He encourages us all the more: "Call upon Me in the day of trouble; I will deliver you, and you shall glorify Me" (Psalm 50:15).

But God's command to pray is more than that of a parent asking a child to tell about her day. First, He wants us to unburden ourselves by telling Him all our worries. God doesn't have to guess at what we're going to say; He knows our trouble, our sin, our fears, and our need for Him better than we ourselves know. Even as we are praying the words, He has already prepared His answer: "Your Father knows what you need before you ask Him" (Matthew 6:8).

Second, when God commands us to pray, He gives us the words to say. Not only is the Lord's Prayer the model of prayer and the actual words that we can say, but all of God's Word can also be a part of our prayers. When commanding us to pray, God is also commanding us to remember what He has already said, who He is, and what He is capable of doing. God gives us wonderful examples of prayer throughout the Scriptures.

Third, God gives power through prayer. James 5:16–18 speaks of this: "The prayer of a righteous person has great power as it is working. Elijah was a man with a nature like ours, and he prayed fervently that it might not rain, and for three years and six months it did not rain on the earth. Then he prayed again, and heaven gave rain, and the earth bore its fruit." None of us consider themselves equal to Elijah, and we likely aren't praying for a three-year drought. But the point of James's words is that the prophet Elijah was heard by the same caring, powerful God who hears us. Pray then with the confidence of Elijah. The power of our prayers is not in our words but in God, who hears us all equally by the grace that is in Christ.

God commands us to pray in every situation. This command steps into the center of every trouble and offers us the help God has already prepared. This command fills our joyful days with the reminder that God is the giver of every good gift and welcomes our thanks. God directs us to pray with the words He has taught us; He promises that those words are as effective for us as they were for the faithful we read about in the Bible.

God's Promises to Listen and Act

"Did you say something? I'm sorry. I wasn't listening."

Those words are said even in the best of relationships. It's no surprise that we often don't listen to one another. We're focused on tasks at hand, thinking of something else, texting, or watching a show. Sometimes when people talk to us, unless they are shouting, we may catch one word in three.

What if the same standard applied to God? What if He didn't listen because He was busy or doing more important things? What if we couldn't pray loudly enough to reach heaven? Would we have any chance of being heard? No. When is God not busy with more important people and problems than ours? And when has our voice ever had volume enough to reach to heaven?

But prayer doesn't depend on our worthiness, importance, or voice. Our prayers depend on God's mercy, His command to pray, and His promises to hear us and act. We're not worthy and never will be, yet He hears us completely, by grace, because He is our Father:

> *Or which one of you, if his son asks him for bread, will give him a stone? Or if he asks for a fish, will give him a serpent? If you then, who are evil, know how to give good gifts to your children, how much more will your Father who is in heaven give good things to those who ask Him! (Matthew 7:9–11)*

Like a loving father who hears and responds to the needs of his children, God certainly knows our needs and has prepared for them. When we worry about the basic necessities of life, hear Jesus' words:

> *Therefore do not be anxious, saying, "What shall we eat?" or "What shall we drink?" or "What shall we wear?" For the Gentiles seek after all these things, and your heavenly Father knows that you need them all. But*

seek first the kingdom of God and His righteousness, and all these things will be added to you. (Matthew 6:31–33)

When we fear that we aren't important enough, God in His Word promises that His attention to us is even greater than that of a mother and her child:

Can a woman forget her nursing child, that she should have no compassion on the son of her womb? Even these may forget, yet I will not forget you. Behold, I have engraved you on the palms of My hands. (Isaiah 49:15–16a)

God uses the best examples of the relationship of parent and child to assure us that His devotion to us is even greater. And since God knows us as the perfect father knows his children, He promises that He also knows what we're going to say. All our words and thoughts are open to Him.

O LORD, You have searched me and known me! . . . Even before a word is on my tongue, behold, O Lord, You know it altogether. (Psalm 139:1, 4)

Therefore, we needn't try to hide any part of our lives from God. No sin is too horrible to confess. No sorrow is too small to express. When we've finished telling Him all we've said and done, God truly can say, "I know."

We might think that since God knows everything, there's no need to tell Him anything. However, He is a Father who loves His children and welcomes them. The parable of the persistent widow gives us this encouragement: "And He told them a parable to the effect that they ought always to pray and not lose heart" (Luke 18:1). The widow goes to the unrighteous judge day after day, but he refuses to hear her. Then, finally, he listens to her, but only to save himself from her coming. Jesus says God is the opposite of the judge. "And will not God give justice to His elect, who cry to Him day and night? Will He delay long over them? I tell you, He will give justice to them speedily" (Luke 18:7–8a).

Our Father welcomes us as His children. Just as a parent loves to hear his children, so God loves our words. He tells us to pray always, not only to receive the gifts He has prepared but also to grow in our relationship with Him. As we obey His command to pray and repeat His own words in our prayers, our faith in Him increases.

This growth in faith comes as we recognize that God hears our prayers beyond what our dearest friends or loving parents can do. Our friends care for us and our parents certainly side with us, but they can only do so much. They can't go into the class with us when we take the test or lie on the operating table during surgery. They can't sit beside us during the job interview and give us the right answers. Friends and family love and listen and advise, but that's their limit.

God listens to our prayers in a way that exceeds any effort by a loved one or friend. He doesn't say, "Call on Me, and I'll see what I can do." He doesn't say, "Call Me, and though I'm busy, I'll see if I can work you in." Rather, He says, "Call upon Me in the day of trouble; I will deliver you, and you shall glorify Me" (Psalm 50:15). The Lord of heaven hears your smallest whisper and deepest fear. He hears you with the heart of a Father and with divine power to provide what you need. He has already proven His heart for us: "He who did not spare His own Son but gave Him up for us all, how will He not also with Him graciously give us all things?" (Romans 8:32).

Therefore, never let yourself imagine that God wants to help but lacks the power. Never fear that He doesn't care enough to help. His love is proven by the cross of His Son, and His power is shown at the empty Easter tomb.

Because He is the one true God, we pray to Him alone. Most often we speak to Him as our Lord and God. By those titles we address the Trinity—Father, Son, and Holy Spirit. We can pray distinctly to the Father, the Son, or the Holy Spirit, such as when Stephen prayed, "Lord Jesus, receive my spirit" (Acts 7:59). We don't pray to angels or to those who have died as though they were necessary intermediaries between ourselves and God. Jesus Himself is the only mediator between ourselves and God, so we pray in His name. "For there is one God, and there is one mediator between God and men, the man Christ Jesus, who gave Himself as a ransom for all" (1 Timothy 2:5–6). We don't need the intercession of any person in heaven because Jesus Himself speaks for us. "Consequently, He is able to save to the uttermost those who draw near to God through Him, since He always lives to make intercession for them" (Hebrews 7:25). Therefore, we can come to God directly through the mercy and grace shown in Christ. Jesus is the faithful High Priest who was tempted but never sinned and who understands our weakness. In our prayers, we come to Him, fulfilling the invitation of God: "Let us then with confidence draw near to the throne of grace, that we may receive mercy and find grace to help in time of need" (Hebrews 4:16).

What Should We Say in Prayer?

When you go in for a job interview, it would be wonderful if you were given a script and told, "Here, say this and the job is yours." What if every test in school came with the answers printed on the back page and your teacher said to use them? We would actually look forward to interviews and tests if we knew what to say and were certain of the result.

Job interviews and school exams don't work that way, but prayer does. When God commands us to pray, He gives us the words to say and His assurance of the result. With the commands, words, and examples of prayer by people of faith, God gives us everything we need to pray and believe His promises.

The Lord's Prayer is the clearest example of prayer. The disciples asked specifically to be taught to pray (see Luke 11:1), and Jesus responded by giving the Lord's Prayer both as the words to pray and as a model for all prayer. Notice that the Lord's Prayer begins with a focus on God, rather than ourselves, and the confession that He is our Father who hears us even in heaven. We praise Him and His name before we speak of anything else. All the wonderful names of God can be thought of here:

He is the Lord of lords, the Wonderful Counselor, the Prince of Peace, and more.

Then we pray that His kingdom and His will would be accomplished among us, just as they are accomplished in His heavenly realm. His kingdom and will are already at work in our lives and on earth, but we pray that we would see it all the more. In the midpoint of the prayer, we pray for our daily bread, all the necessities of life that our Father already knows we need.

Our most serious need comes when we ask for forgiveness and the ability to forgive others. We ask for forgiveness with certainty that God has already reconciled the world to Himself: "For our sake He made Him to be sin who knew no sin, so that in Him we might become the righteousness of God" (2 Corinthians 5:21). Our forgiveness doesn't depend on how we compare to others or on what we promise to do in the future—it depends on Christ alone. And because we are forgiven, we are able to ask God's help in extending forgiveness to others.

Finally, we call for His protection and for Him to lead us to our heavenly home.

The entire span of heaven and earth and our place in it—past, present, and future—are gathered in these few words of the Lord's Prayer. While we can linger on any petition and add the specifics of particular needs, the Lord's Prayer gives us the overall direction and content of prayer. Because the Lord's Prayer is the prayer Jesus Himself taught us, with it comes the certainty that these are the words God desires to hear and is ready to fulfill.

The Bible provides other examples of prayer, along with God's answers. A striking example is the short prayer of a tax collector in contrast to the long, self-congratulatory prayer of a Pharisee. Jesus described the humble man's prayer:

> *The tax collector, standing far off, would not even lift up his eyes to heaven, but beat his breast, saying, "God, be merciful to me, a sinner!" I tell you, this man went down to his house justified, rather than the other. (Luke 18:13–14)*

This account reminds us that it is by God's grace alone that we are heard at all and that any self-justifying words are useless. Like the tax collector, we can simply confess that we have sinned and are seeking assurance of His forgiveness.

Another biblical model of prayer is Psalm 51. In this psalm, David confesses his sins of adultery and murder. David's cry for mercy and a new beginning speaks for all of us:

> *Hide Your face from my sins, and blot out all my iniquities. Create in me a clean heart, O God, and renew a right spirit within me. Cast me not away from Your presence, and take not Your Holy Spirit from me. (Psalm 51:9–11)*

Our prayers for forgiveness, whether using the Bible's words or our own, have the assurance that God has forgiven us through the work of Christ. We can say with conviction:

> *I acknowledged my sin to You, and I did not cover my iniquity; I said, "I will confess*

my transgressions to the LORD," and You forgave the iniquity of my sin. (Psalm 32:5)

Other biblical models include prayers for the safety and welfare of others:

Give justice to the weak and the fatherless; maintain the right of the afflicted and the destitute. (Psalm 82:3)

We can say prayers of thanksgiving:

Oh give thanks to the LORD, for He is good; for His steadfast love endures forever! . . . This is the day that the LORD has made; let us rejoice and be glad in it. (Psalm 118:1, 24)

We can boldly tell God our feelings when we feel abandoned and distant from Him:

Why, O LORD, do You stand far away? Why do You hide Yourself in times of trouble? (Psalm 10:1)

Times of discouragement are balanced by remembering the nature of God and His acts for the world:

> *Give thanks to the Lord of lords, for His steadfast love endures forever; to Him who alone does great wonders, for His steadfast love endures forever; to Him who by understanding made the heavens, for His steadfast love endures forever. (Psalm 136:3–5)*

Given the richness of the psalms and the diverse lives of biblical people, God gives us a great range of examples of prayer for every situation we may face.

When and Where Should We Pray?

A good relationship is not lacking in communication. Much of it is the ordinary conversation that fills the day, from the first "good morning" to the last "good night." We tell each other about the little things that happen, and we remember to say the six words of a happy relationship: "please," "thank you," and "I love you." So also, in prayer, we acknowledge the wonderful relationship God makes with us. Prayer can be the first words of our morning and our last peaceful thoughts at night. By our prayers, we recognize God's presence with us every moment and the gifts with which He surrounds us. There's no single time to pray, so every time is fitting. Paul wrote:

> *Rejoice always, pray without ceasing, give thanks in all circumstances; for this is the will of God in Christ Jesus for you. (1 Thessalonians 5:16–18)*

While we can pray at any moment about anything, some times are especially appropriate to speak to our heavenly Father. The start of the day is an excellent time to give thanks for the night's sleep and to ask for God's direction in the new day. Likewise, prayer in the evening is a wonderful way to close the day, giving thanks for His gifts and commending our worries to His care. It's fitting to give thanks for our food before and after each meal. It's right to pray when a group is gathered to make a crucial decision or to begin an important project. Before you start a trip, pray for God's care, and as you arrive at your destination, give thanks for your safety. In short, any event can be the impetus for prayer.

Since we're prompted to pray by the routine events of the day, it means we pray everywhere. Also, some places especially inspire us to pray and are appropriate for longer, more involved prayers. The church building is one such place. The beauty, the quiet, the reminders of the promises of God depicted in stained glass windows—all these make the church sanctuary a natural place to pray. We might remember the words of Solomon when, in the dedication of the temple in Jerusalem, he described the temple and the prayers of the people: "Listen to the plea of Your servant and of Your people Israel, when they pray toward this place. And listen in heaven Your dwelling place, and when You hear, forgive" (1 Kings 8:30). Many go to worship services early, linger after the service, or visit the sanctuary outside of scheduled services for the opportunity to meditate on God's promises and to pray.

Besides the church sanctuary, other places move us to pray. Jesus directed His disciples to pray privately in their rooms:

> *But when you pray, go into your room and shut the door and pray to your Father who is in secret. And your Father who sees in secret will reward you. (Matthew 6:6)*

We also pray in difficult places. Paul and Silas were praying and singing hymns while they were held as prisoners in the jail in Philippi. At midnight, while singing and praying, God opened the prison doors for them (Acts 16:25–26). The example of Paul and Silas is good to remember when your own fears try to imprison you in a night of worry. Other places to pray are at gravesides, in hospital rooms, and in dangerous places. Remember the invitation of Peter: "Casting all your anxieties on Him, because He cares for you" (1 Peter 5:7).

Morning or night, in church or at home, it's always the time and place to pray.

Should Our Prayers Follow a Set Form?

There are many patterns suggested for prayer. Types of prayer include confession of our sin, thanksgiving for forgiveness and all gifts, requests for wisdom and growth in faith and service, and intercession for the welfare of others. There is no single sequence that must be followed, but some acronyms are helpful reminders to broaden the content of our prayers. For example, A.C.T.S. stands for *adoration*, *confession*, *thanksgiving*, and *supplication*. P.R.A.Y. stands for *praise*, *repent*, *ask*, and *yield*.

Another useful form of prayer is that of the collect, the short prayer that is common in worship. The collect addresses God by a specific name and quality, since it's because of God's promises to help us that we come to pray at all. For example, we can recall God's promise to give wisdom to all who ask, so we ask that God give us the wisdom to choose the course He intends for us, that He bring a blessing through that wisdom, and that we give thanks for it. These short prayers are a wonderful combination of the promises of God, our requests, and the blessings God desires to give.

Patterns vary according to the needs of the day. Sudden changes within our family and circle of friends or the needs of our world might reorder our prayers greatly from one day to the next. Such change reminds us that our prayers are not only for ourselves but also for all people. We can pray for those we know and for the stranger who crosses our path. The needs of all are known to God, and He holds them in the same love that He gives us.

How Long Should We Pray, and How Does God Answer Prayer?

The simple answer to the first question is to pray until God answers you, keeping in mind that the length of time does not dictate the length of our prayer. Jesus warns "they think they will be heard because of their many words (Matthew 6:7). We read in the Bible the prayers of those who were ill and called out to Jesus for healing; they then gave thanks when they were healed. That direct, brief model of prayer is definitely possible when God chooses to give an answer quickly and in a way that is easily seen.

However, there is more to God's answer than an immediate result. Part of God's answer is in the act of prayer itself. We have noted Luke 18:1 already: "And He told them a parable to the effect that they ought always to pray and not lose heart." We pray not only to receive God's gifts but also to exercise the gift that is prayer. We pray as a reminder that we are in our Father's hands. Our place there is more important than the gifts we receive from Him. When we pray, God gives us patience and trust in Him. While we're praying for healing, a job, greater peace in the family, or any other tangible thing, God is already answering our prayer by hearing us and drawing us closer to Himself through our dependence on His promises.

Besides the immediate response of listening to our prayers and promising to provide for us, God might answer our prayers in the time and manner we desire. Many were healed immediately when they appealed to Jesus. But God might also delay the answer, drawing us further into prayer and closer to Himself. This scenario is like the extended conversation Jesus had with the Syrophoenician woman who asked for help for her daughter (see Mark 7:24–30) and the forty days of prayer and travel Elijah endured before God's answer on the mountain (see 1 Kings 19:4–18). If you don't immediately get what you pray for, don't despair—rather, keep praying with trust in God's will.

Nevertheless, be prepared for an answer that is different from the one you seek. Paul prayed three times that God would remove the thorn in his flesh; God's answer was not the removal of the trouble but the strength to bear it. The greater change came within Paul, who said, "Therefore I will boast all the more gladly of my weaknesses, so that the power of Christ may rest upon me" (2 Corinthians 12:9). While we naturally want our troubles taken away, God's answer might be the strength needed to endure. Paul explained this truth:

> *God is faithful, and He will not let you be tempted beyond your ability, but with the temptation He will also provide the way of escape, that you may be able to endure it. (1 Corinthians 10:13)*

Perhaps the clearest directions concerning the content and length of prayer come in Philippians 4, when Paul says:

> *Do not be anxious about anything, but in everything by prayer and supplication with thanksgiving let your requests be made known to God. And the peace of God, which surpasses all understanding, will guard your hearts and your minds in Christ Jesus. (Philippians 4:6–7)*

Our worries prompt us to pray. God says, in essence, "Tell Me what you are worried about." He wants us to tell Him at length what He already knows. He listens as does no one else in the world. He invites us to ask for His gifts and answers to our worries. That is our supplication. When those requests are made, it's time for thanksgiving. We can give thanks to God for what He has already done, what He is doing right now, and for what He has prepared for the future. Long before we're done giving thanks, His peace comes to guard our hearts and minds.

Conclusion

What a gift God has given us in the bridge that is prayer! He gives us strong commands to pray, along with the assurance that He welcomes our words and hears them all. His Word reminds us that He answers us with wisdom, love, and power that we find nowhere else. Our prayers can be the exact words of the Lord's Prayer, examples of other biblical prayers and psalms, or prayers in the Divine Service. Or we can simply tell Him our concerns and repeat His promises to listen and to care. While we pray, His answers already come as we remember His words and know that He cares for us and all for whom we pray. We're blessed to carry out these directions:

Rejoice always, pray without ceasing,

give thanks in all circumstances; for this is the will of God in Christ Jesus for you. (1 Thessalonians 5:16–18)

Morning Prayer

I thank You, my heavenly Father, through Jesus Christ, Your dear Son, that You have kept me this night from all harm and danger; and I pray that You would keep me this day also from sin and every evil, that all my doings and life may please You. For into Your hands I commend myself, my body and soul, and all things. Let Your holy angel be with me, that the evil foe may have no power over me. Amen.

Evening Prayer

I thank You, my heavenly Father, through Jesus Christ, Your dear Son, that You have graciously kept me this day; and I pray that You would forgive me all my sins where I have done wrong, and graciously keep me this night. For into Your hands I commend myself, my body and soul, and all things. Let Your holy angel be with me, that the evil foe may have no power over me. Amen.